Paul Mealor

REQUIEM
'THE SOULS OF THE RIGHTEOUS'

for SATB choir, percussion and strings

(2018)

Vocal score

NOVELLO

First performed on 22 September 2018 at St Mary's Episcopal Cathedral, Edinburgh by the National Youth Choir of Scotland and the Royal Scottish National Orchestra, conducted by Christopher Bell.

INSTRUMENTATION

SATB choir
Wine glasses*

Percussion (3 players):
Crotales
Wind Chimes
Glockenspiel
Tubular Bells
Suspended cymbal
Timpani

Strings

*A selection of the choir play pre-tuned wine glasses pitched at D, F, F sharp and A.

Duration: *c.* 40 minutes

Full Score: NOV297242
Vocal Score: NOV297242-01
Parts are available on hire from the publisher.
www.musicsalesclassical.com

CONTENTS

I.   Requiem aeternam: The Souls of the Righteous 1

II.   The Beatitudes 12

III. Kyrie Eleison..19

IV. Gloria 21

V.   The hand that held the knife 31

VI. Sanctus and Benedictus 36

VII. Blessed is the Stranger 41

VIII. Agnus Dei 46

IX. If Ye Love Me 49

X.   Lux aeterna: And let there be a Heaven 51

TEXTS

I

Requiem aeternam dona eis, Domine,
Et lux perpetua luceat eis.
(Eternal rest grant unto them, O Lord,
And let perpetual light shine upon them.)

Introitus from the Requiem Mass

The souls of the righteous are in the hands of God,
but who is righteous only God can say.
Our grace and grief are gathered to the night,
and darkness may be wiser than the day.

The souls of the righteous are in the hands of God,
but what the soul is only God can know.
When those we loved are taken from our sight,
let them be going homewards when they go.

The souls of the righteous are in the hands of God,
but where is God to make the broken whole?
The love that holds us, right or wrong,
is in the scarred hands of the righteous soul.

Grahame Davies

II

Blessed are the poor in spirit: for theirs is the kingdom of heaven.

Blessed are they that mourn: for they shall be comforted.

Blessed are the meek: for they shall inherit the earth.

Blessed are they which do hunger and thirst after righteousness: for they shall be filled.

Blessed are the merciful: for they shall obtain mercy.

Blessed are the pure in heart: for they shall see God.

Blessed are the peacemakers: for they shall be called the children of God.

Blessed are they which are persecuted for righteousness' sake: for theirs is the kingdom of heav'n.

Blessed are ye, when men shall revile you, and persecute you, and say all manner of evil against you falsely, for my sake.

Rejoice, and be exceeding glad: for great is your reward in heav'n: for so persecuted they the prophets which were before you.

Gospel according to Matthew 5:12

III

Kyrie eleison. Christe eleison. Kyrie eleison.
(Lord have mercy. Christ have mercy. Lord have mercy.)

IV

Gloria in excelsis Deo, et in terra pax hominibus bonae voluntatis. Laudamus te, benedicimus te, adoramus te, glorificamus te. Gratias agimus tibi propter magnam gloriam tuam. Domine Deus, Rex caelestis, Deus Pater omnipotens. Domine Fili unigenite, Jesu Christe. Domine Deus, Agnus Dei, Filius Patris, qui tollis peccata mundi, miserere nobis. Qui tollis peccata mundi, suscipe deprecationem nostrum. Qui sedes ad dexteram Patris, miserere nobis. Quoniam Tu solus Sanctus, Tu solus Dominus, Tu solus latissimus, Jesu Christe. Cum Sancto Spiritu, in Gloria Dei Patris. Amen.

(Glory be to God on high, and in earth peace, goodwill towards men. We praise thee, we bless thee, we worship thee, we glorify thee, we give thanks to thee, for thy great glory. O Lord God, heavenly King, God the Father Almighty. O Lord, the only-begotten Son, Jesu Christ; O Lord God, Lamb of God, Son of the Father, that takest away the sins of the world, have mercy upon us. Thou that takest away the sins of the world, receive our prayer. Thou that sittest at the right hand of God the Father, have mercy upon us. For thou only art holy; thou only art the Lord; thou only, O Christ, with the Holy Ghost, art most high in the glory of God the Father. Amen.)

V

To those who have walked in the shadows of war.
Bring peace, bring peace.

For the hand that held the knife, a scarred hand to forgive.
Bring peace, bring peace.

The faithless and the faithful, the traitor and the true.
Bring peace, bring peace.

No question to answer, no price to pay.
Bring peace, bring peace.

Home when the day is over, or home when dawn is grey.
Bring peace, bring peace.

Grahame Davies

VI

Sanctus, Sanctus, Sanctus, Dominus Deus Sabaoth.
Pleni sunt coeli et terra Gloria tua. Osanna in excelsis.
(Holy, holy, holy, Lord God of Hosts.
Heaven and earth are full of thy Glory Glory be to thee, O Lord Most High.)

Benedictus qui venit in nominee Domini. Osanna in excelsis.
(Blessed is he that cometh in the name of the Lord. Hosanna in the highest.)

VII

Blessed is the stranger in the street;
Blessed the beloved at the door;
Blessed the ally and the enemy;
Blessed are the powerful and the poor.

Blessed are all ways you come to us,
and all the faces that you take,
Blessed the grace and grief you bring;
Blessed the hearts you heal and those you break.

Blessed the faith, and blessed the fear;
Blessed the warrior, blessed the weak;
Blessed the peace, blessed the pain;
Blessed the lost and blessed who seek.

Show your salvation, blind though we may be, come in all things and give grace to see.

Grahame Davies

VIII

Agnus Dei, qui tollis peccata mundi, miserere nobis.
Agnus Dei, qui tollis peccata mundi, miserere nobis,
Agnus Dei, qui tollis peccata mundi, dona nobis pacem.
(O Lamb of God, that takest away the sins of the world, have mercy upon us.
O Lamb of God, that takest away the sins of the world, have mercy upon us.
O Lamb of God, that takest away the sins of the world, grant us thy peace.)

IX

If ye love me, keep my commandments.
And I shall pray the father,
and he shall you another comforter,
that he may abide with you forever;
Even the spirit of the truth.

Gospel according to John 14:15–16

X

And let all those who leave our company,
together or alone,
find the strange road
they follow takes them home.

And let there be a heaven
for those who find their way through hell,
and let there be forgiveness
for those who broke before they fell.

A mystery all the greater for the answer,
a darkness all the deeper for the star,
a sunlight all the purer for the shadow,
a beauty made more perfect by the scar.

Grahame Davies

Lux aeterna luceat eis, Domine.
Cum sanctis tuis in aeternum, quia pius es.
(Let eternal light shine upon them, Lord,
with your saints in eternity, because You are Holy.)

Communio from the Requiem Mass

Requiem: The Souls of the Righteous

A mass to commemorate the centenary of the end of the First World War, 1918-2018

Mass settings
with additional poetry by Grahame Davies

PAUL MEALOR

I – Requiem aeternam: The Souls of the Righteous

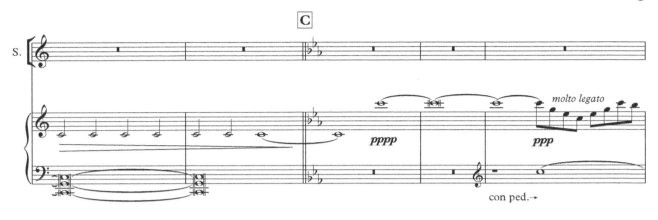

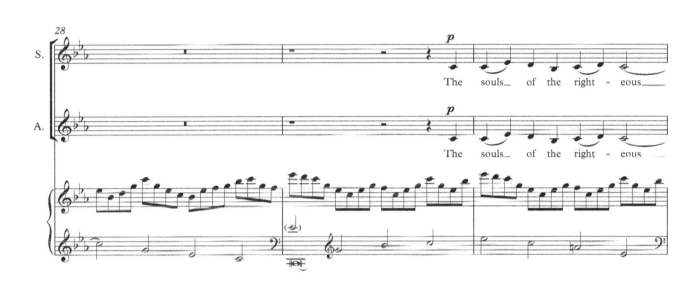

4

5

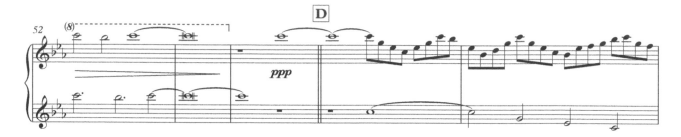

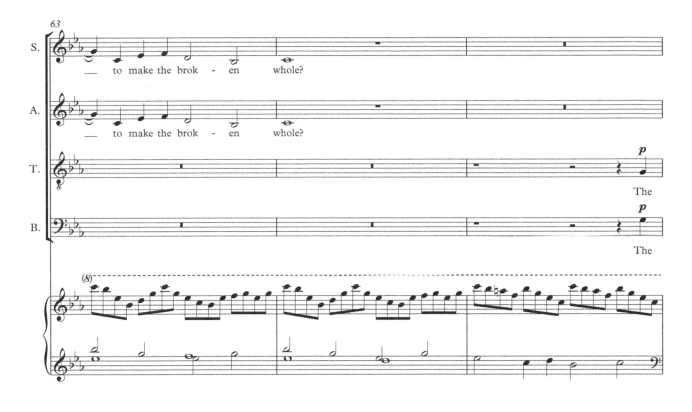

to make the brok - en whole?

to make the brok - en whole?

The

The

The love that holds us, right or wrong,___ is in the scarred hands of the

The love that holds us, right or wrong,___ is in the scarred hands of the

love that holds us, right or wrong,___ is in the scarred___ hands___ of the right - -

love that holds us, right or wrong,___ is in the scarred___ hands___ of the right - -

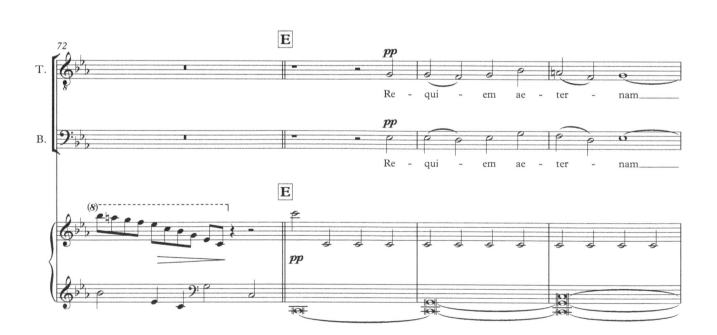

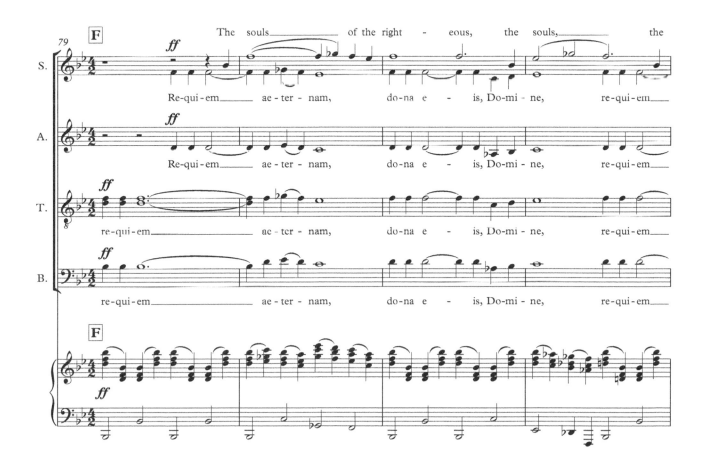

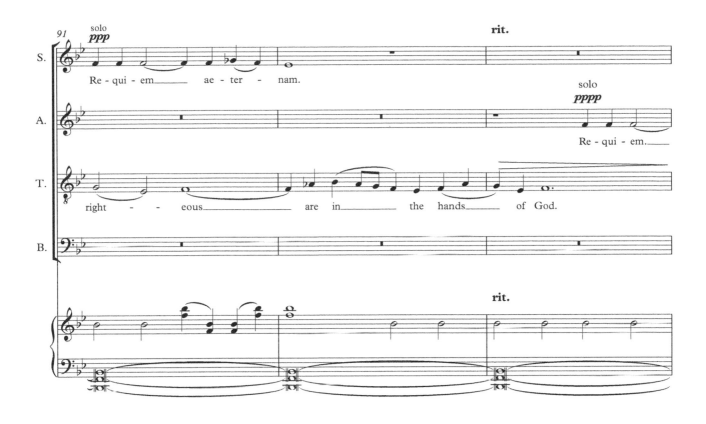

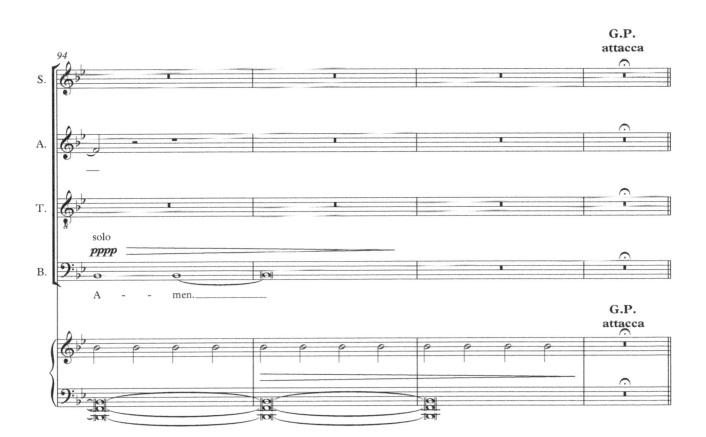

II – The Beatitudes

Bless - ed are the meek: for they shall in - he - rit the earth.

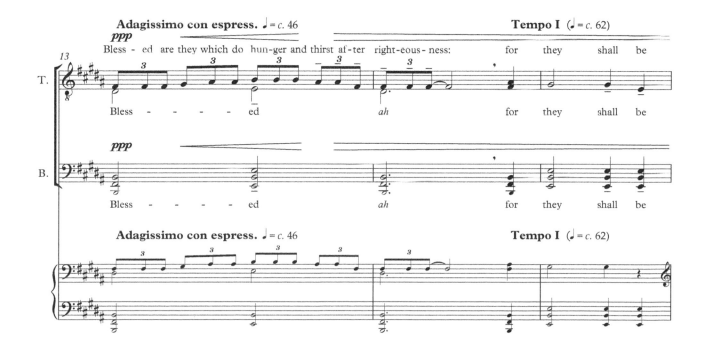

Bless-ed are the mer-ci-ful: for they shall ob-tain — mer - cy.

Bless-ed are the mer-ci-ful: for they shall ob-tain mer - cy.

filled.

filled.

filled.

Bles-sed are the pure in heart: for they shall see God.

Bles-sed are the pure in heart: for they shall see God.

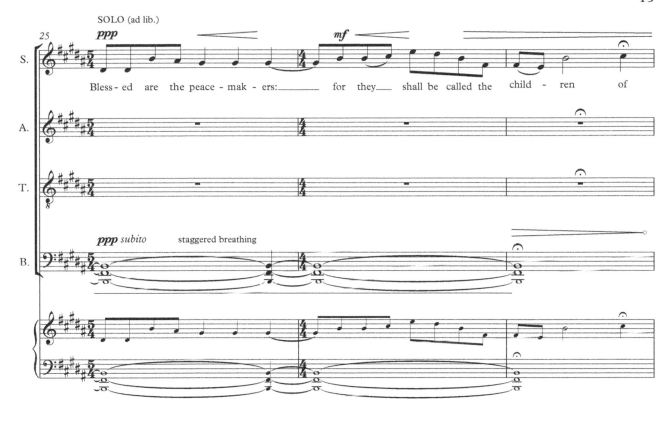

16

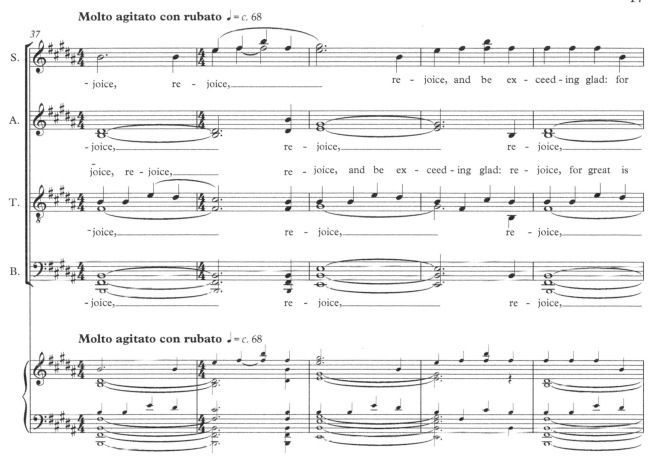

III – Kyrie Eleison

20

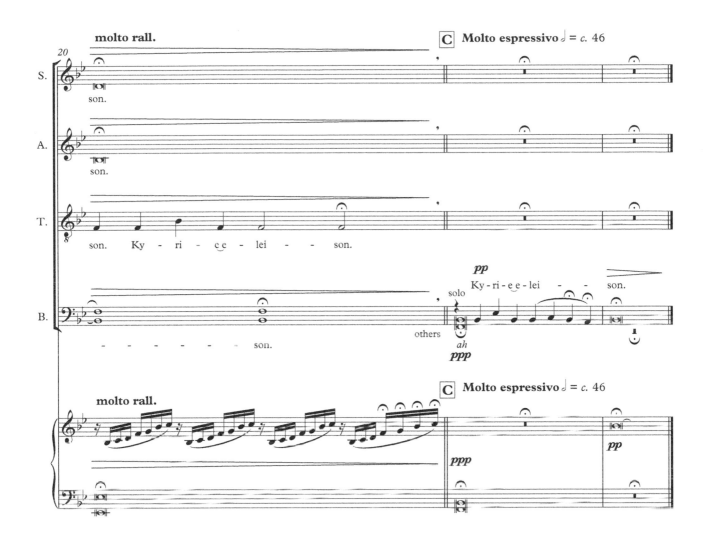

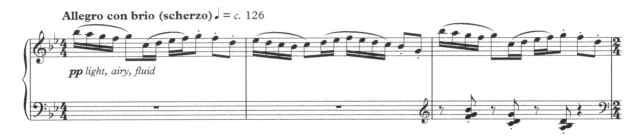

IV – Gloria

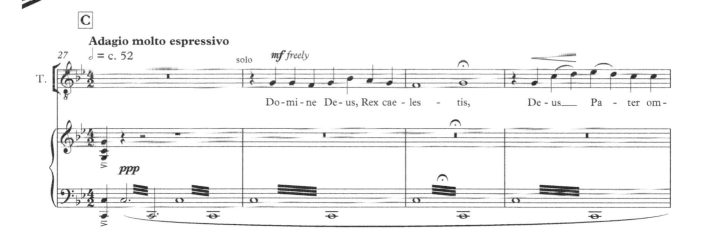

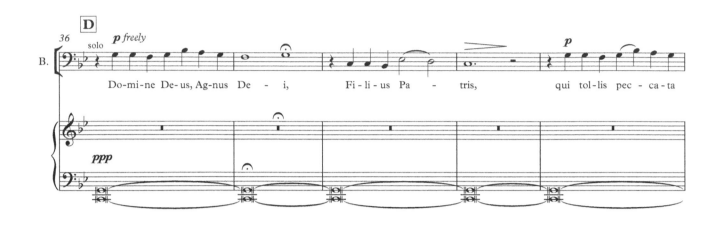

Do-mi-ne De-us, Ag-nus De - i, Fi - li - us Pa - tris, qui tol-lis pec - ca - ta

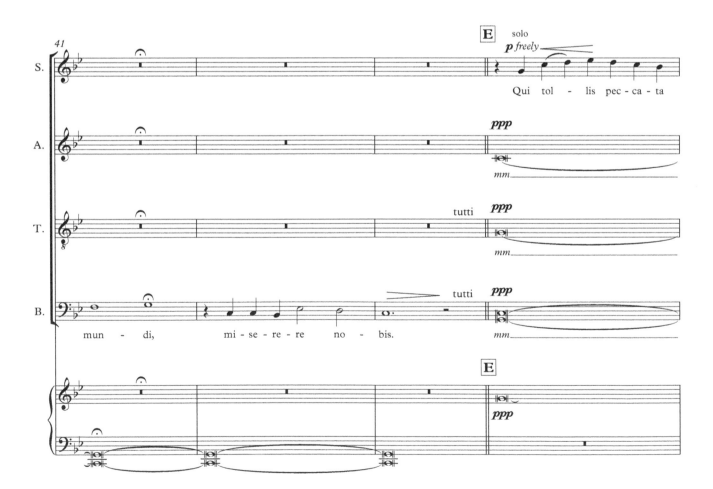

Qui tol - lis pec - ca - ta

mun - di, mi - se - re - re no - bis. mm

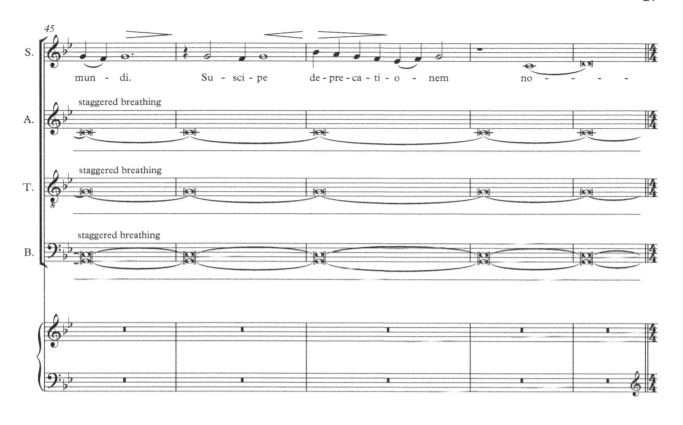

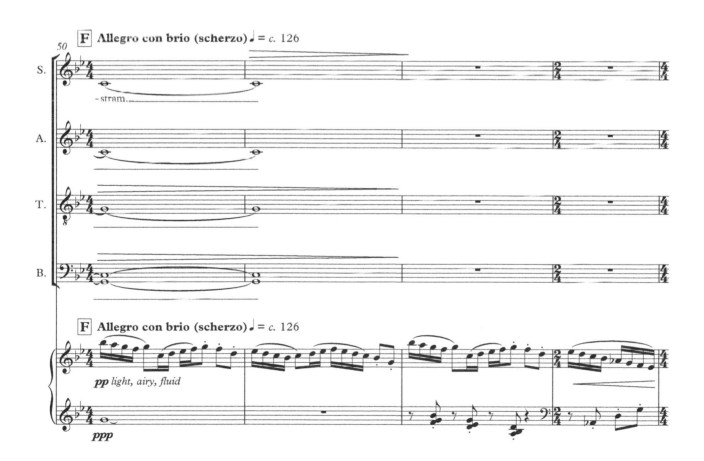

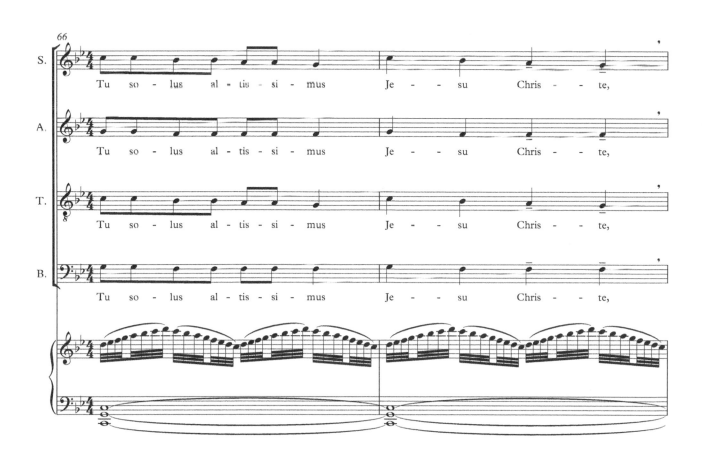

V – The hand that held the knife

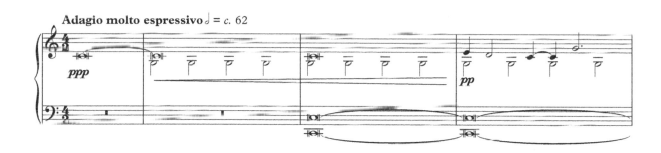

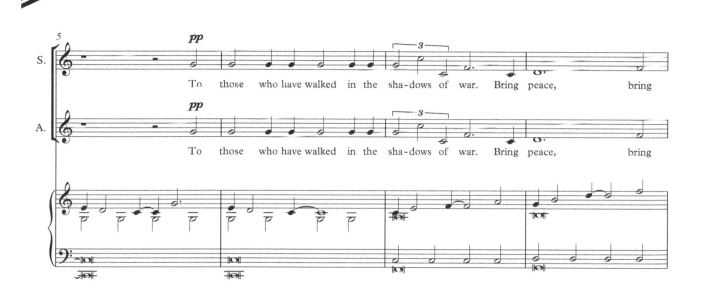

34

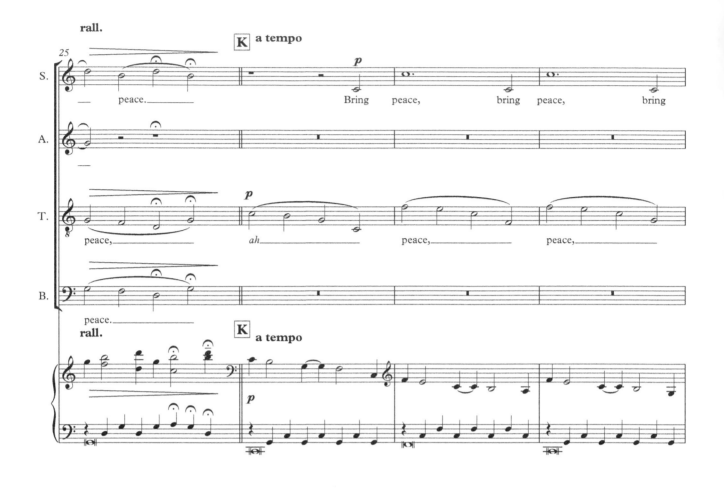

VI – Sanctus and Benedictus

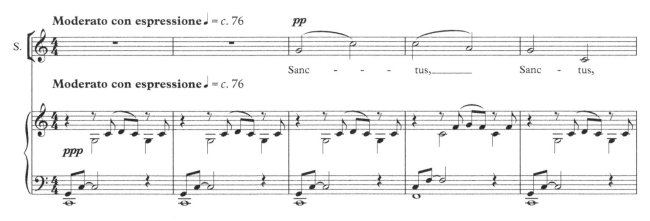

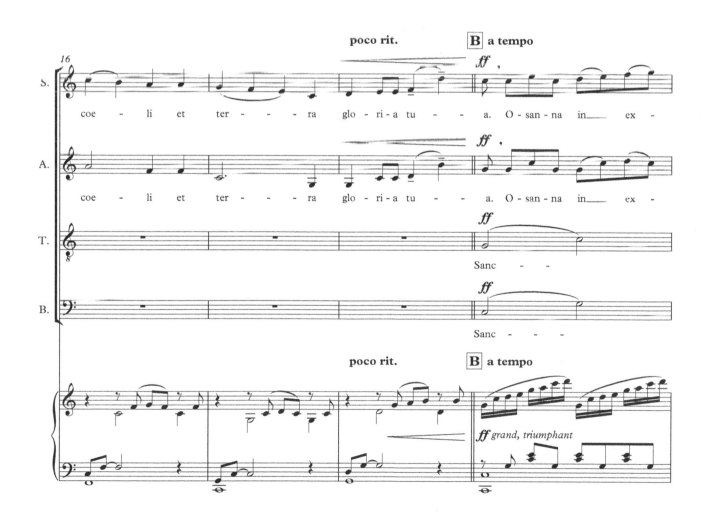

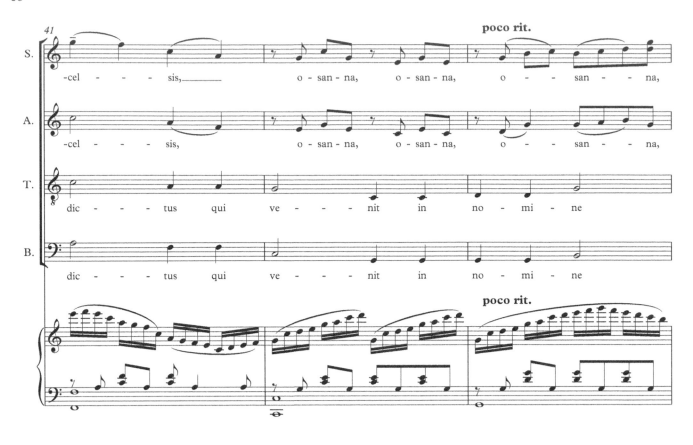

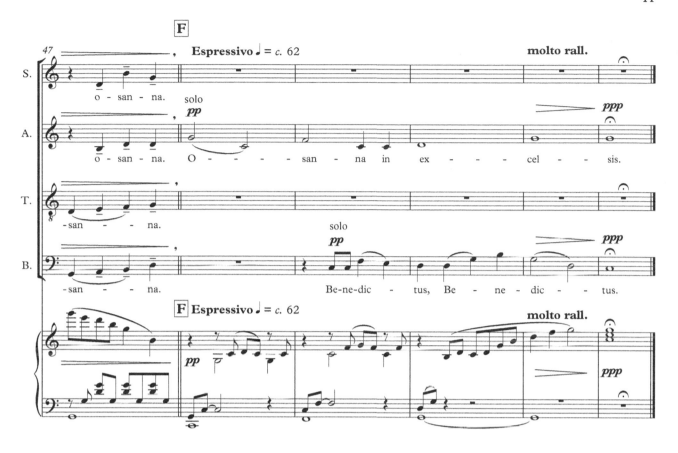

VII – Blessed is the Stranger

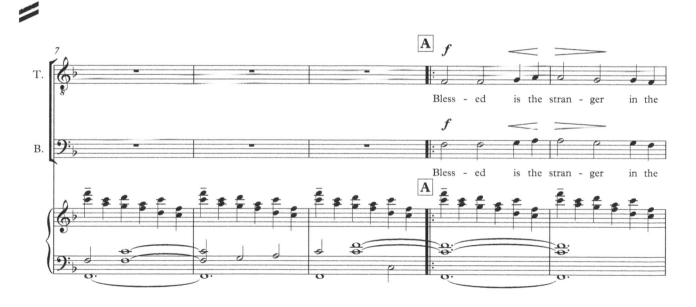

44

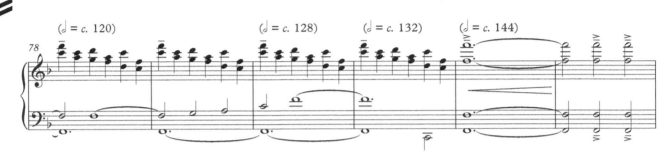

VIII – Agnus Dei

IX – If Ye Love Me

SMALL GROUP OF OFF-STAGE SOPRANOS

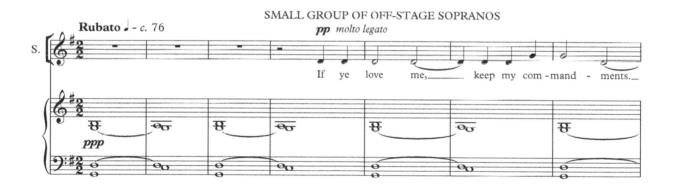

X – Lux aeterna: And let there be a Heaven

* A selection of the tenors and basses should play pre-tuned
  wine glasses, by rubbing their fingers over the wine rim.

52

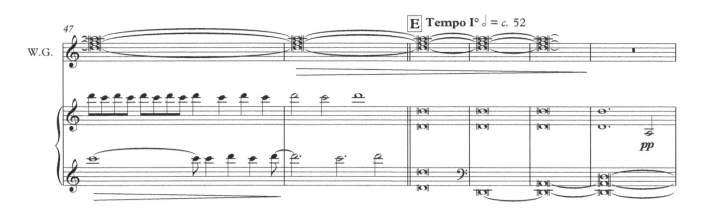

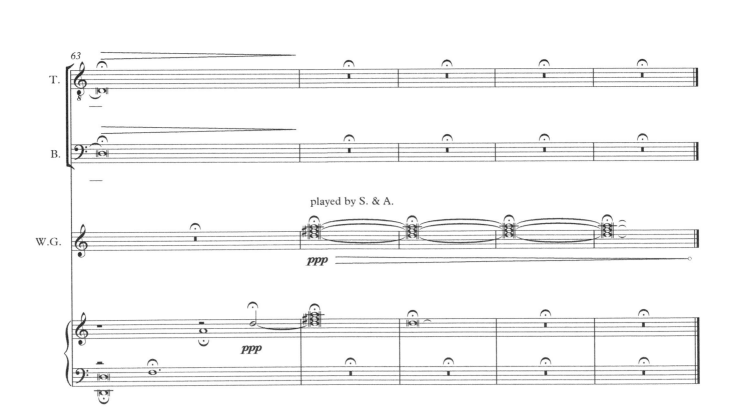

played by S. & A.